A Road Connects Places

Connects Places

Crystal Sikkens
Crabtree Publishing Company
www.crabtreebooks.com

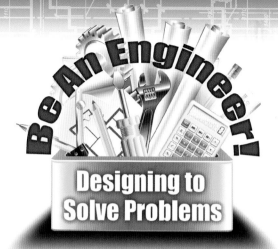

Be An Engineer!

Designing to Solve Problems

Author: Crystal Sikkens

Series research and development:
   Janine Deschenes and Reagan Miller

Editorial director: Kathy Middleton

Editor: Petrice Custance

Proofreader: Kathy Middleton

Design and photo research: Katherine Berti

Print and production coordinator: Katherine Berti

Images:

Getty Images: Bloomberg: p. 15

Shutterstock
   Joseph Sohm: p. 16 bottom right
   Peter Moulton: p. 17

The Canadian Press Images
   Montreal Gazette—John Mahoney: p. 19

All other images by Shutterstock

Library and Archives Canada Cataloguing in Publication

Sikkens, Crystal, author
      A road connects places / Crystal Sikkens.

(Be an engineer! Designing to solve problems)
Includes index.
Issued in print and electronic formats.
ISBN 978-0-7787-5161-8 (hardcover).--
ISBN 978-0-7787-5165-6 (softcover).--
ISBN 978-1-4271-2109-7 (HTML)

      1. Roads--Design and construction--Juvenile literature. 2. Roads--
Juvenile literature. 3. Highway engineering--Juvenile literature. I. Title.

TE175.S55 2018   j625.7'25   C2018-902995-1
                                              C2018-902996-X

Library of Congress Cataloging-in-Publication Data

Names: Sikkens, Crystal, author.
Title: A road connects places / Crystal Sikkens.
Description: New York, New York : Crabtree Publishing Company,
   [2019] | Series: Be an engineer! Designing to solve problems |
   Includes index.
Identifiers: LCCN 2018027876 (print) | LCCN 2018029209 (ebook) |
   ISBN 9781427121097 (Electronic) |
   ISBN 9780778751618 (hardcover : alk. paper) |
   ISBN 9780778751656 (pbk. : alk. paper)
Subjects: LCSH: Roads--Design and construction--Juvenile literature.
Classification: LCC TE175 (ebook) | LCC TE175 .S47 2019 (print) |
   DDC 625.7--dc23
LC record available at https://lccn.loc.gov/2018027876

Crabtree Publishing Company

www.crabtreebooks.com   1-800-387-7650

Printed in the U.S.A./092018/CG20180719

Published in Canada
Crabtree Publishing
616 Welland Ave.
St. Catharines, Ontario
L2M 5V6

Published in the United States
Crabtree Publishing
PMB 59051
350 Fifth Avenue, 59th Floor
New York, New York 10118

Published in the United Kingdom
Crabtree Publishing
Maritime House
Basin Road North, Hove
BN41 1WR

Published in Australia
Crabtree Publishing
3 Charles Street
Coburg North
VIC 3058

Contents

Hi, I'm Ava and this is Finn. Get ready for an inside look at the world of engineering! The Be an Engineer! series explores how engineers build structures to solve problems.

After reading this book, join us online at Crabtree Plus to help us solve real-world engineering challenges! Just use the Digital Code on page 23 in this book.

Pothole Problem

Dakota lives out in the country. Rain and snow often flood her street and damage the road. Traffic wears down these weak spots until they collapse. These potholes make the drive to school slow and bumpy. Dakota wondered how to fix this problem.

Maybe, she thought, there is a way to drain the water from the road so it won't flood. Or, they could stop vehicles from using the road when it is soft and wet.

The Best Solution

The more Dakota thought about the problem, the more she began to wonder if the best solution might be to build a new road. A road is a long stretch of land whose surface is made smooth. Vehicles use roads to travel from one place to another.

Did you know?

Not all roads are the same. City roads, **rural**, or country, roads, and highways are all built differently. An area's traffic, **environment**, and the materials available nearby determine what kind of road is built.

What Is an Engineer?

First, Dakota used her problem-solving skills to come up with ways to fix the holes in her road. She was thinking just like an engineer! An engineer is a person who uses math, science, and creative thinking to design things that solve problems and meet needs.

Different Engineers

Different kinds of engineers work at finding solutions to different problems. Some look for ways to improve **communication**, food, or medicines. Others design and oversee the building of roads and other structures. Often different engineers work together to solve the same problem.

Many engineers are involved in building a road. Some design and build it. Other engineers work to keep the environment and the animals around the road safe.

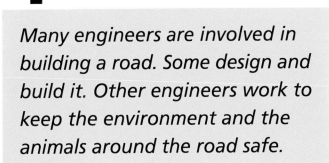

Steps to Finding Solutions

To make sure their solutions are both safe and **effective**, all engineers follow the same set of steps when solving problems. This set of steps is called the Engineering Design Process. These steps are often repeated many times to find out which solutions will work and which will not.

The Engineering Design Process

1 ASK
Ask questions and gather information about the problem you are trying to solve.

2 BRAINSTORM
Work with a group to come up with different ideas to solve the problem. Choose the best solution.

3 PLAN AND MAKE A MODEL
Create a plan to carry out your solution. Draw a diagram and gather materials. Make a **model** of your solution.

4 TEST AND IMPROVE
Test your model and record the results. Using the results, improve, or make your design better. Retest your improved design.

5 COMMUNICATE
Share your design with others.

Asking Questions

In order to find a solution to the problem of potholes in the road, an engineer starts by asking questions and gathering information. The answers will help explain why the holes are forming. This is the first step in the Engineering Design Process.

An engineer might study the type of weather that is common in the area, how much traffic uses the road, or the types of vehicles that might be on it.

Brainstorming

Next, an engineer brainstorms, or talks with others about ways to solve the problem. He or she might use a diagram like this one to help organize their ideas.

Problem

Potholes continue to form on the road.

Don't let heavy vehicles, such as trucks and tractors, use the road.

Put up a fence to help keep blowing snow off the road.

Create **ditches** beside the road for rainwater and melted snow to drain into.

Build a new road with a different surface material. Build up one side of the road so water runs off to the side.

Planning

If the solution chosen is to build a new road, the engineer will start by gathering information about things such as the weather, traffic, and cost. He or she decides what size the road will be, how water will drain off, what kind of **foundation** it needs, and what material to use on the surface. The main materials are earth, chipseal, concrete, and asphalt.

Earth roads are made from dirt or loose stones called gravel. They are easy and inexpensive to build. Earth roads are used in rural areas.

*Chipseal roads are made from mixing gravel with asphalt or **tar**. This kind of covering is called pavement. This is the least expensive kind of paved road. Chipseal is usually used in rural areas.*

Roads paved with concrete are used where there is a lot of traffic and heavy vehicles. Concrete roads cost more to build, but they last a long time. They are used for city roads and highways.

Some city streets and highways are paved with asphalt. This material can be **recycled** and is cheaper than concrete. Asphalt roads are quicker to build and repair, but they do not last as long.

Creating a Model

An important part of an engineer's job is to make sure a road design is safe for drivers. One feature an engineer might add to a winding road is **guardrails**. Guardrails are railings that stop vehicles from going off the road. To test the design of a guardrail, an engineer will create a model of it. A model is a **representation** of a real object.

*A model can be a **3-D** object or a drawing on a computer. Models can help engineers explain their design to the builders.*

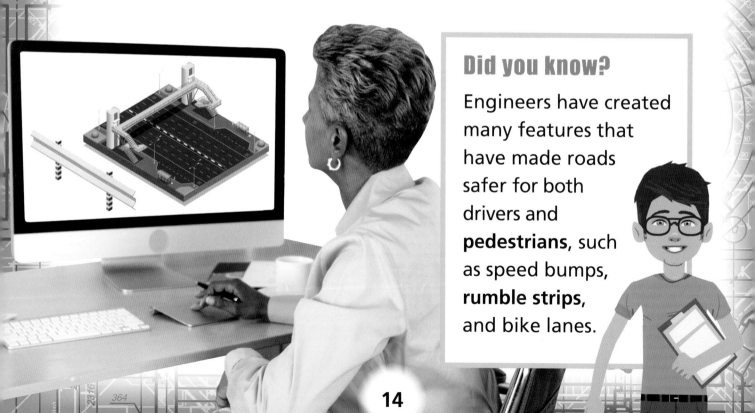

Did you know?

Engineers have created many features that have made roads safer for both drivers and **pedestrians**, such as speed bumps, **rumble strips**, and bike lanes.

Testing and Improving

Testing a model of a guardrail will show whether it will hold back vehicles of different sizes the way it has been designed. A test will also show whether a vehicle might flip over the guardrail or slide under it when it is hit.

Based on the results of each test, engineers can adjust the design of the guardrail and retest it if necessary.

Sharing the Results

After each test, the engineer records the results. These results are then shared with others who can give feedback, or opinions, on what could be changed or improved. Sharing results helps future engineers build stronger, safer roads all around the world.

Information from the past helps today's engineers create roads that last longer, drain better, are less slippery, and stand up under heavy traffic.

Making Improvements

Ever since the invention of the first vehicles, engineers have been working to make roads safer and easier to use. Today, people can drive across water on bridges or underneath through tunnels. Painted paths across the road, called crosswalks, show pedestrians where to cross safely. Some roads have lanes just for bikes to keep them safe from cars.

Did you know?

A company in Idaho called Solar Roadways has been working on roads made with **solar panels**. The panels would use sunlight to light up crosswalks and melt snow.

Some roads with a lot of traffic have a round roadway, known as a traffic circle, to keep vehicles moving.

Important Steps

A road is designed to last for a certain number of years. The Engineering Design Process is important in helping engineers find out how the road will hold up to heavy traffic, weather, and changes in the environment now and in the future.

To keep drivers safe, engineers must check roads regularly to find out whether they need repairs or improvements.

Part of the De La Concorde overpass in Canada collapsed on September 30, 2006.

Road Collapse

The De La Concorde **overpass** in Quebec, Canada, was built in 1970. The engineers' design did not plan for an increase in traffic and heavier vehicles over the years. The road was designed to last 70 years. Unfortunately, it collapsed after only 36 years from the extra weight of the vehicles.

Model Activity

To decide on the path a new road should take, engineers must study the **landforms** of the area, such as hills and lakes. They need to figure out the safest path for the road to follow. Try it yourself. Build a model of an area with landforms. Then, figure out how a road could cross it safely.

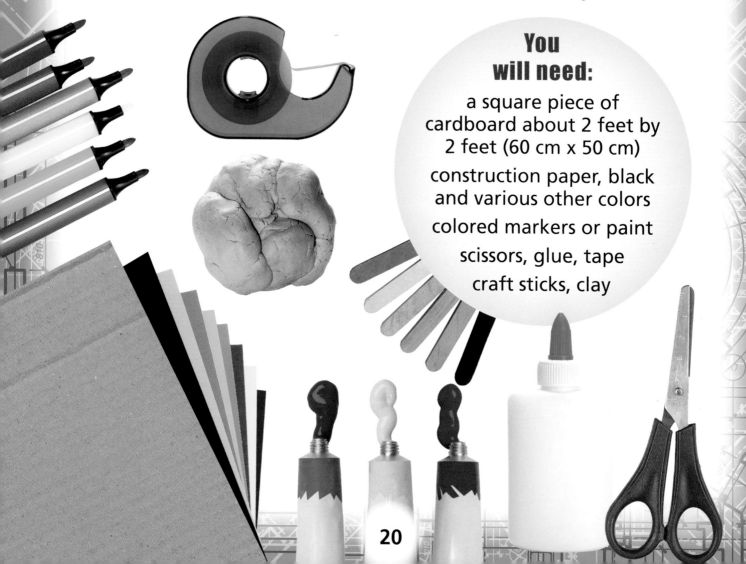

You will need:

a square piece of cardboard about 2 feet by 2 feet (60 cm x 50 cm)

construction paper, black and various other colors

colored markers or paint

scissors, glue, tape

craft sticks, clay

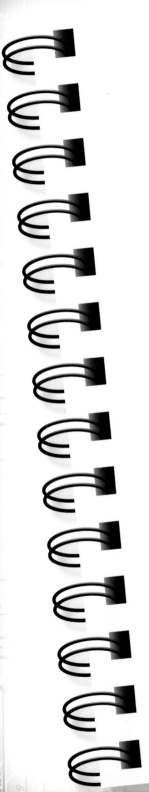

Instructions:

1. Using paint, colored markers, and construction paper, draw at least one body of water, such as a lake or an ocean, that takes up one-quarter of the cardboard square.
2. Next, use the clay to add one mountain that is 4 inches (10 cm) wide at the bottom.
3. Then, using the materials listed, add other landforms to your model, such as hills, rivers, plains, and canyons.
4. Once your landscape model is dry, add a road across it using black construction paper. The road must go from one corner to the other. If your road is going over a body of water, use the craft sticks to build a bridge.

Did your road have to go through any tunnels?

Why do you think the path you chose for your road is the safest route?

Avoiding Disaster

The collapse of the De La Concorde overpass was a hard reminder of how important it is to follow the steps in the Engineering Design Process. Proper research, planning, and testing helps engineers build safe new roads. Just as important, it also helps them to strengthen, repair, and improve roads after they are built.

Building a safe road on a mountain can be challenging. Do some research and find out why the steps in the Engineering Design Process can help avoid a disaster on a mountain road.

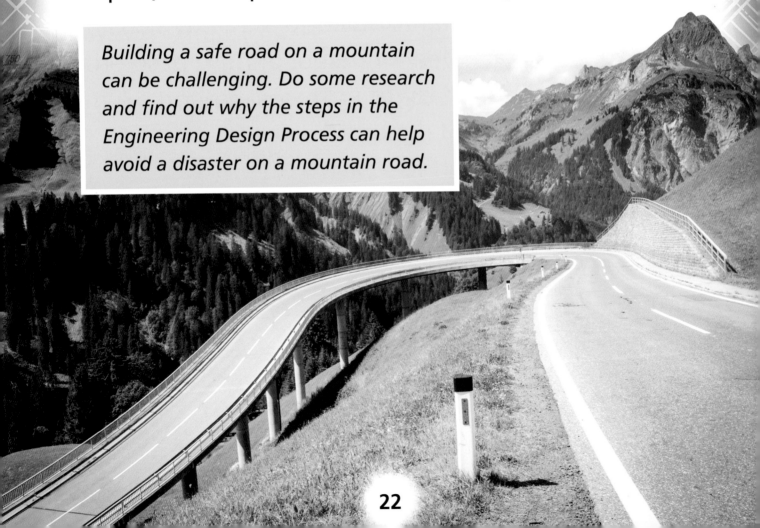

Learning More

Books

Bernhardt, Carolyn. *Engineer It! Road Projects* (Super Simple Engineering Projects). Super Sandcastle, 2017.

Peppas, Lynn. *Road Makers and Breakers* (Vehicles on the Move). Crabtree Publishing Company, 2012.

Polinsky, Paige V. *Roads* (Engineering Super Structures). Sandcastle, 2017.

Websites

This website gives you information about how to build a road, as well as some fun activities to try: **https://wonderopolis.org/wonder/how-do-you-build-a-road**

Find out more about the different construction vehicles used to build a road at: **www.wdbridge.com/en/how-a-road-is-built#kids-zone-scene-5-tooltip-1-details**

For fun engineering challenges, activities, and more, enter the code at the Crabtree Plus website below.

www.crabtreeplus.com/be-an-engineer

Your code is:
bae04

Glossary

Note: Some boldfaced words are defined where they appear in the book.

3-D (THREE-DEE) *adjective*
Short for three-dimensional, an object that has length, width, and height

communication (kuh-myoo-ni-KEY-shuhn) *noun* The act of sharing thoughts, opinions, or information

ditch (dich) *noun* A long, narrow hole dug in the ground, usually alongside roads, used for draining water

effective (ih-FEK-tiv) *adjective* Producing the correct result

environment (en-VAHY-ern-muh-nt) *noun* The natural surroundings of things

foundation (foun-dey-SHUN) *noun* The ground or base something is built on

landform (LAND-fawrm) *noun* A natural feature found on Earth's surface

model (MOD-l) *noun* A representation of a real object

overpass (OH-ver-pas) *noun* A road that crosses above another road

pedestrian (puh-DES-tree-uhn) *noun* A person who travels on foot

recycled (ree-SAHY-kuh-ld) *adjective* Treated or processed to be used again

representation (rep-ri-zen-TEY-shun) *noun* Something that stands in place for something else

rumble strip (RUHM-buhl strip) *noun* A set of raised or rough strips of pavement used to slow vehicles down

solar panels (SOH-ler PAN-ls) *noun* Materials specially made to convert the Sun's energy into electricity

tar (tahr) *noun* A dark, thick liquid made from wood or coal, which hardens

A noun is a person, place, or thing. An adjective is a word that tells you what something is like.

Index